Holy Week

Holy Week

A Spiritual Guide
from Palm Sunday to Easter

Emil Bock

Floris Books

Translated by Alfred Heidenreich
Edited by Tony Jacobs-Brown

This volume is an extract from *The Three Years*,
originally published in German under the title
Die Drei Jahre by Verlag Urachhaus in 1946.

First published in English in 1955 by The
Christian Community Press, London.
Fifth, revised edition published in 2005 by
Floris Books.

The New Testament passages are from *The
New Testament, A Rendering* by John Madsen,
published in 2000 by Floris Books.

British Library CIP Data Available

ISBN: 978-086315-790-5

Printed in Poland

Contents

Foreword

The Week of Weeks, or Holy Week, is the climax and focus of the gospels. Five of the sixteen chapters of the Gospel of St Mark are devoted to this one week. The events later in that week have been lived through and re-enacted by countless Christians through the centuries. The Lord's Supper or Eucharist, which in The Christian Community is celebrated as the Act of Consecration of Man, connects us to one of its central events.

One of the founders of The Christian Community, Emil Bock, saw a need for a renewal of theology to go alongside the renewal of religious life which is this movement's central purpose. Fired by the spiritual investigations of Rudolf Steiner and his own wide reading of the occult and mythological traditions, Bock illumined the great cosmic pictures of the gospels. He wrote a series of books on the Old and New Testament. Buried deep within the volume, *The Three Years: The Life of Christ Between Baptism and Ascension,* is a chapter on Holy Week. Here we find the spiritual and cosmological background for the events that unfolded in this crucial week. Bock's explanations satisfy the need of modern human beings not only to *feel* deeply the pathos and grandeur of what is described, but to *understand* the events in order to penetrate to deeper layers of meaning.

Bock's approach is at once clear and poetic. He loves to give the widest perspective, soaring like an eagle above what he surveys, allowing the underlying contours of the landscape to become visible, even if sometimes the detail is unclear. He also shows the interest of a true pastor, drawing out the moral direction that can be taken from the events, although he never does this in a moralising way.

Bock never intended his work to be the final word. He maintained a dialogue with modern theological and archaeological investigations, and would surely have integrated the many results of this research that have been produced in the more than half a century since he completed *The Three Years*. Still it seems worthwhile to make his work accessible to a new generation without making major changes, for this would mean rewriting it entirely. Perhaps one detail can be added to, for it makes the picture in many ways more subtle and more revealing. This concerns the identity of the crowds present on Palm Sunday and Good Friday. Bock's descriptions imply that there was only one crowd in Jerusalem, which was present on both occasions, crying 'Hosanna' on Palm Sunday and 'Crucify him!' on Good Friday. However, there is strong evidence that the population of Jerusalem swelled many times over in the week before Passover, growing from around 80,000 to as many as 250,000. It is quite conceivable that different groups from this huge number were present on the different days of Holy Week. What is revealed is not necessarily the fickleness of individuals, but the phenomenon of the 'crowd' which can enlist individuals in a higher recognition or in a deadly rejection.

To Bock's writing we have added extracts from the gospels for each day. The translation chosen is Jon Madsen's which is perhaps closest to Bock's own translation of the New Testament into German.

Rev Tom Ravetz, November 2010

Introduction

The week before Easter is not only a significant and exceptional period in the Christian year, it is important also in the cycle of nature. In the Christian year, the whole drama of the Passion is enacted in this space of time, and its events form the grand conclusion of the gospel. In various regions of Christendom it is called not only Holy Week, but also the Great Week. Only those able to experience its greatness can fully participate in the festival of Easter.

In nature's year this week before Easter is important because the spring full moon occurs in it. The spell of winter is finally broken; by leaps and bounds the new life of the earth goes forward. In the equinoctial conflict of day with night day gains the victory, which is consolidated in the triumph of light on the first Sunday after the vernal full moon.

The events of Holy Week, as related in the gospel, do not harmonize at first with spring in nature. On the contrary, they stand in sharpest contrast to it. Only at the very end, when the Easter sun has risen, the festival of rejoicing harmonizes with the exultation of spring. The solemn drama of Holy Week is the preparation for this harmony. The springtime of nature comes about of itself. The inner spring of the Easter festival must be achieved by the path of pilgrimage which passes along the stations of Holy Week.

The seven days before Easter can be compared with the Twelve Holy Nights of Christmas. This period 'between the years' is the right preparation for the

twelve months of the New Year for everyone who con-
templates the inner meaning of midwinter. On those
who inwardly participate in the mystery drama of
the Passion the seven days of Holy Week bestow new
forces for the whole of their future destiny.

The events which happened two thousand years
ago were providential prototypes. Through them
the seven days of each week have taken on new
meaning. The names of the seven days of the week
in the European languages show that they reflect
the qualities of the seven planetary spheres. Thus
we have the sun (Sunday), moon (Monday), Mars
(Tuesday, French: mardi), Mercury (Wednesday,
French: mercredi), Jupiter (Thursday, French: jeudi),
Venus (Friday, French: vendredi), Saturn (Saturday).
In that one week before Easter, at the end of the life
of Jesus, each weekday was stamped anew with a
Christian planetary aspect, over and above the cosmic
differentiation.

Christendom at present has little understanding
of the content of the days of Passion Week. Certainly,
on Good Friday thoughts are turned to the cross on
Golgotha, and in some parts of Christianity every
Friday is marked as a fast day. But beyond this no
striking picture has been attached to any day except
Palm Sunday, which in some countries is celebrated
with a display of palm branches. In reality, however,
each of the seven days reveals a cosmic secret in
human and historical form.

At the entry of the Christ into Jerusalem on Palm
Sunday, the sun of the past, the old sun, stood again

royally in the heavens. Nevertheless it was about to receive its dismissal, for the new sun, the Easter sun, was to rise on the following Sunday. When on the Monday Christ cursed the fig tree and cleansed the Temple in the holy city, his encounter was with the moon-forces of the ancient world which needed renewal. On the Tuesday, it was the Mars spirit which Christ bent to his purpose. For on the Tuesday of that week Christ was in conflict with his opponents, who came forward group after group in the hope of trapping him in his teaching. The Christ's weapon was the spirit-word; finally, in the echo of the conflict, he retired with the disciples to the Mount of Olives and revealed to them an apocalyptic view into the future. On the Wednesday, in the anointing at Bethany and in the betrayal of Judas, Mercury encountered the Christ-sun. And as on Maundy Thursday Christ washed the disciples' feet and administered the sacrament to them, there shone a Jupiter light, full of future promise, in the sorrow of their souls. On Good Friday all that has ever been granted to man by the goddess of love, Venus or Aphrodite, was most wonderfully transmuted and enhanced. A deed of love was done on that day greater than all other possible deeds of love. Love's sacrificial death on Golgotha was the transformation of the Venus-principle through the sun-principle of Christ. As the body of Christ rested in the grave, the Christ-sun met the Saturn-spirit in the universe; until finally Sunday brought the octave, and the sun itself rose in the heavens, the Christ-sun which had fought its way through all these stages.

The sacred drama of Holy Week is a complete artistic whole. Having grasped the value of stages in the life of Jesus, one can perceive in this drama the secret of its composition. For what takes place in the seven days before Easter is a concentration of Christ's life as a whole. The same archetypal laws, and the progress from stage to stage, which were manifested in the sacred biography of the three years, are repeated in dramatic brevity. In the light of Holy Week the three years of the complete life of Christ can be recognized as one great Passion.

Matthew 21:1–11

The entry into Jerusalem

And they approached Jerusalem and came to Bethphage by the
Mount of Olives. Then Jesus sent two disciples ahead ²and said
to them, Go to the village which you see before you. There you
will straight away find an ass tied, and a colt with her. Untie
them and bring them to me. ³And if anyone says anything to
you, then say: The Lord needs them. Then he will let you take
them at once.' ⁴The word of the prophet was to be fulfilled:

    ⁵Say to the daughter Zion:

    See, your king comes to you in majesty.

    He rides on an ass and on the foal of the beast of burden.

    ⁶The disciples went and did what Jesus had told them; ⁷they
brought the ass and the colt and laid their garments on them
and he sat on them. ⁸Many in the crowd spread their clothes on
the road, others cut branches from the trees and strewed them
on the road. ⁹And the crowds which went before him and followed him called out loudly:

    Hosanna, sing to the Son of David!

    Blessed be he who comes in the name of the Lord!

    Sing to him in the highest heights!

    ¹⁰As he entered Jerusalem in this way, the whole town was
stirred and said, 'Who is he?' ¹¹And the crowd said, 'It is Jesus,
the prophet from Nazareth in Galilee.'

Palm Sunday

Christ enters the holy city on the first day of Holy Week. It is at first an unpretentious sight. He rides through the gate of the city upon an ass, followed by his faithful believers. But suddenly, as though he were the god of spring himself, his entry creates a frenzy in the souls of the people. It is as though the crowd were seized with the ecstasy of a pagan spring festival. Primitive rites are revived when the people cast down palm branches from the trees. The palm has always ranked as the tree-symbol of the sun which shines in the spring sky with renewed strength. The crowd spread his path with the symbol of the sun. Is he in fact perhaps the friend and lord of the sun who has been promised to man as the great king of the light? Is the original spiritual significance of the city of Jerusalem to be released from enchantment, the city which sheltered on Mount Zion one of the oldest sun-sanctuaries of humanity, before it was overshadowed by Mount Moriah, the Mount of the moon, with the Temple of Solomon? Has the time of Melchizedek, the great sun-initiate, come back?

It would appear as though the Christ had now really found entrance into humanity. The high sun-spirit has already lived for three years in a human body and undergone earthly destiny. He held back and kept silence; and whenever he stepped forward he was met with hostility and lack of understanding. Is all this now to take a new direction? Is destiny to find a solution in an ecstatic jubilation?

No, this is the beginning of the most solemn week
in human history. The same men who strew palms
and break forth into fervid Hosannas will shriek with
fanatical hatred a few days later: 'Crucify him! crucify
him!' The cross on Golgotha, the symbol of death, will
companion the palm branch, the symbol of life. It is
Christ himself who brings about the sudden reversal
of feeling. He passes through the ecstatic crowd in
silence, with grave countenance. He sees through the
acclamations; they are merely superficial, and he aims
at deeper levels. His will is directed to something very
different.

One might ask why Jesus did not stay in Galilee,
in his home, especially at the time when the country
round the Sea of Galilee blooms in all the miraculous
colours of spring? Yes, if he had stayed in Galilee he
would have remained alive. But one might just as
well ask: Why did not Christ remain as a god in the
heavenly worlds? His whole being found its meaning
in making this renunciation. To make his entry into
Jerusalem, knowing that in so doing he threw down
the gauntlet to his enemies, was to complete his entry
into the earthly world. The events of the first day of this
solemn week corresponded, on another level, to those
that had marked the inception of his earthly path. As
at that time he forsook the heavens, so now he forsakes
the glory of Galilee. It made no stir among men as
Christ descended from the heavenly spheres to earth.
Even John the Baptist, who played the role of priest at
this entry into earth existence, scarcely noticed anything of what took place as Jesus of Nazareth became

bearer and vessel of the Christ. But it was proclaimed in the spheres above humankind. The words rang out: 'This is my beloved Son in whom I am well pleased.' And on Palm Sunday, in this strange hour of ferment and exaltation, the event is acclaimed by men. The Hosanna of the ecstatic mob corresponds to the word which once sounded out of spiritual heights. Suddenly the people feel that he who comes riding on the ass's foal is not merely man. It is as though the folk-soul broke through and perceived the shining radiance, the sun-aura, that blazed forth from the figure of Jesus. For three years the divine nature of Christ had had to hold back, or it would have overwhelmed men with its power. But now this holding back bears its fruit. The divine element, which had sacrificed itself in humility to the human, is transformed into powerful resolution of the will. To begin with, the divine in him radiated through the human; but now the human nature is consumed in the fire of God. It is this scintillating fire of the will which scatters kindling sparks among the crowd. The people are seized with the presentiment of a revolutionary Passover feast, but they can only take it to mean a political springtide of the nation.

The Christ knows better. Into the holy city, that quintessence of the whole pre-Christian evolution of humanity, he bears something which is different from everything that earth can bring forth from herself. It is a seed which must change the world from the very foundations. The reaction may seem like a tremor of assent, but a few days more and it is plain that this superficial mood can curse as easily as bless. The earthly vessel into which Christ entered at the baptism can ultimately bring him only death. The city which cries Hosanna can at last only nail him to the cross.

The spark springs across, but the Christ goes calmly through the waves of enthusiasm and acclamation. He will make his entry on deeper levels. How wonderful is the sun when it rises in the morning and brings the day to birth. Yet this external sun with which man as a natural being is connected sets again each evening. When the height of summer has passed, it withdraws from the earth and its strength fades away. So it is with human life; at some moment of time each of us must die, no matter how vivacious we were in childhood and youth. Palm Sunday is the day of the old sun, the natural sun; Easter Sunday will be the day of the new sun, the spiritual sun. This spiritual sun does not set; it is steadfast and enduring. It can, moreover, be found more easily in times of difficulty, indeed, in sickness and death, than in happiness or in the carefree days of childhood. Christ enters the old Jerusalem on Palm Sunday, but he carries the new Jerusalem into the setting, dying world. Christ desires to kindle the new sun, which is steadfast, true and omnipresent deep within the earth and humankind. This is the way that leads from Palm Sunday to Easter Sunday, from the old sun to the new.

The story of the entry into Jerusalem shows how insufficient all ecstatic conditions are. It is certainly right that we should be joyful in the glory of spring, when we are among children and when we encounter youth and love. This natural enthusiasm assuredly must not be rejected.

But it is dangerous if it is mistaken for the reality of life. Purely natural enthusiasm springs from the body only; it touches the level of the spirit only for fleeting moments. True enthusiasm, one that does not rapidly pass from the Hosanna to the crucify, is not formed from below upwards, but from above downwards. True enthusiasm is born when the spiritual takes root in human nature; when the spark of the spirit comes to earthly realization and incarnation.

Mark 11:12–25

The fig tree

[12]And on the next day when they left Bethany again, he felt hunger. [13]And from a distance he saw a fig tree in full leaf, and he went to see if he could find fruits on it. And when he came up to the tree he found nothing but leaves; and indeed it was not the season for figs. [14]And in response he said to the tree, 'Never again in any age to come shall anyone eat of your fruits!' And his disciples heard these words.

Cleansing the Temple

[15]And they came to Jerusalem. And he went into the Temple and he began to drive out those who sold and those who bought in the Temple; he overturned the tables of the money-changers and the chairs of those who sold doves, [16]and he did not allow vessels to be carried through the Temple. [17]And he taught them and said, 'Is it not written:

> My house shall be called a house of prayer among all
> peoples?

But you have made it a den of robbers.' [18]When the chief priests and the scribes heard this, they wondered how they might destroy him. They were afraid of him because all the people were enraptured by his teaching. [19]And when evening came he went out of the town.

[20]In the morning when they passed by they saw that the fig tree had withered right down to its roots. [21]Then Peter remembered and said to him, 'Master, see! The fig tree which you cursed has withered.' [22]And Jesus said to them, 'Through the power of faith you can unite with God. [23]Yes, I say to you: Whoever then shall say to this mountain: Rise up and throw yourself into the sea, and has no doubt in his heart but rather is confident that his word will be effective, he will experience that it will happen. [24]Therefore I say to you: Everything towards which you direct

Monday in Holy Week

There is a certain quiet place which even today is shrouded in mystery. It is upon the road which every morning and every evening of Holy Week was traversed by Jesus and his disciples, whether leaving the city for Bethany in the evening or returning to Jerusalem in the morning. Crossing the summit of the Mount of Olives, coming from Jerusalem, and slowly descending the other side towards the valley, where from the depths of the Judean wilderness glitters the sub-earthly mirror of the Dead Sea, one comes to a spot surrounded by high walls. It lies halfway between the Mount of Olives and Bethany. Black cypresses rise above the walls and point heavenward like solemn beacons. In the time of Jesus there was a little settlement here, Bethphage, the House of Figs. This village was not like other villages. A group of persons led there a life in common, united by a special spiritual tie. The simple huts in which they probably dwelt were surrounded by a hedge of fig trees which gave the place its name. These fig trees, however, were not mere bearers of fruit; they were sacred to the people who lived there, visible symbols of their special training for the spirit. These were people who sought to preserve in their circle a spiritual mystery of the past, the same mystery which is hinted at in the story of Nathanael. The group at Bethphage cultivated a condition of supersensory sight which was called 'sitting under the fig tree.' It was attained by means of meditative exercises, supported partly by special postures of the body.

the power of prayer in your inner striving will be granted to you, if only you have full confidence that you can achieve it.

[25] 'But when you prepare to pray, if you are holding a grudge in your heart against anyone, first forgive; then your Father who is in the heavens can also forgive you your strayings.'

It was from Bethphage that in the early hours of
Palm Sunday Jesus instructed Peter and John to fetch
the ass and her colt. For just as there were trees there
which were held as sacred, so too were these animals.
The asses kept there were no beasts of burden; they,
too, symbolized a mystery. The memory still lived of
the magician Baalam who was called from Babylon
to curse the Israelites and prevent them from enter-
ing the Land of Promise. Baalam was pictured in the
Old Testament as riding on an ass. But it was known
that the phrase had a hidden meaning: it referred to
a definite state of soul. It was really a somnambulent
withdrawal from consciousness in which formerly
the Babylonian magician began to speak. Baalam
spoke out of a kind of spiritual possession, not from
his human consciousness, and without his knowing
how it came about the magic curse which he was to
utter became a blessing instead. The sacred animals
harboured at Bethphage indicate that the supersensory
vision cultivated there was somnambulistic and bound
to the physical body. Right into modern times the ass
often appears in fairy tales as the imaginative repre-
sentative of the physical human body.

The ass's colt upon which Christ rode into the holy
city on Palm Sunday belongs to the realm of memo-
ries associated with Bethphage. But as he rode boldly
into the city on the sacred white beast, there was no
repetition of the Baalam condition of 'riding on the
ass;' it was the crowd who, beholding him, fell into
the ecstatic withdrawal from ordinary consciousness.
It was as though a language of Baalam gripped the

people as they cried Hosanna to the one who rode
upon the ass's colt.

When the day drew towards evening, Jesus went to
Bethany with his disciples to rest, as also on the following days. In the night the echo of popular ecstasy with
its Hosannas echoed in his soul. And when next morning they passed by Bethphage on the way to Jerusalem,
neither he nor his disciples remained unchanged by
what had taken place. There was something deeply
earnest in the bearing of the Christ, something inexo-
rable. Then comes the enigmatic approach to the fig
tree. The disciples wondered why Jesus should expect
to gather figs, when it is not their season. And they
heard him speak the strangely harsh words: 'Never
again shall fruit ripen on you in all ages.' Perhaps they
dimly felt in this moment that something greater lay in
the words than just a statement about the tree and its
fruitfulness. But the scales did not fall from their eyes.

And now in Jerusalem the disciples pass a day with
the Christ in which many dramatic scenes follow each
other. As their Master sets foot on the threshold of the
Temple precincts, chaos breaks out. Everywhere there
is panic and terror; tables are overturned, money rolls
across the ground. It is a reversal of the ecstatic jubilation of yesterday.

Then the night is again spent at Bethany, and
the next morning Jesus and his disciples come by
Bethphage at dawn. There the sight of the withered
tree suddenly confronts them, and the disciples ask
Jesus to explain it to them. It was no crude miracle, as
though Jesus through his angry word of power had

robbed a creature of its existence. How could he have destroyed a tree belonging to the people who had willingly placed at his disposal the ass and the ass's colt! No, it was a spiritual act, denoting an important moment in the mystery of Holy Week.

The signal for the decisive battle had already been given through the awakening of Lazarus. But it was on Palm Sunday that the full being of the Christ was revealed and it was this that stirred men's souls. But this moment had also its simple human meaning. Jesus, as other devout people, was going to the Temple for prayer and sacrifice in preparation for the Passover. But a foreboding of great decision had seized him. Things could no longer go on painlessly, as in the past. The Christ sees that mere enthusiasm is superficial and untrustworthy, but as yet he is not constrained to repulse it. That he cannot directly reprove the people is shown next day by a similar scene before the Temple. This time it is children who cry out Hosanna. When his enemies ask maliciously, 'Do you hear what they are saying?,' he replies, 'Yes, have you never read: By the mouth of children and newborn infants I am praised?' (Matt.21:16).

But now the night at Bethany has come between and there is a certain contrast with the mood of Palm Sunday. He approaches the fig tree at Bethphage and wishes to show the disciples how little value should be attached to the Hosanna of the previous day. All that it represented was the last fruits of the old visionary clairvoyance, given by nature, and bound to the body. The words he addresses to the fig tree are, as it were, a

challenge to the whole realm of ancient ecstatic vision.
Here a momentous decision is made in the history of
humanity. Jesus rejects the Hosannas of the people,
and himself brings about the transition to their cry,
'Crucify him.' He has the courage himself to summon
the spiritual blindness through which the people will
fanatically demand his death. Humanity must act out
of a consciousness that leads to freedom, even if it
means tragedy; even if men in their spiritual blindness
nail him on the cross.

When the fig tree of Bethphage is seen again by
the disciples on the morning of Tuesday, a wholesome
disenchantment has come over them. They see the
withered tree, just there on the spot which they have
always treated with veneration. They receive teaching
from Jesus which serves as a prelude to what they will
hear from him in the evening hour on the Mount of
Olives. Then they are led to realize that some day there
will be a new sight for humankind, and that faith is to
be the germ of this. Jesus says to his disciples: 'Yes, I say
to you, if you have the power of faith without waver-
ing, then you will not only bring forth the fruit of the
fig tree, but you will be able to say to this mountain:
Rise up and throw yourself into the sea, and it will be
so.' There will be no barrier before you; the mountain
of the sense world which bars your sight will disap-
pear. Through the rocky stone of earthly existence you
will see the true nature of things permeated by divine
thought. The power of faith will bring to maturity in
the human heart the eye of the new vision. The Sermon
on the Mount speaks of this: 'Blessed are the pure in

heart, for they shall see God.' But in between the old moon-vision, no longer serviceable, and the new sun-like vision of the heart, there lies a time of darkness, of blindness to the spirit. And in this stage of blindness Christ will be nailed on the cross.

On that Monday in Holy Week Christ rejects a temptation. Had he allied himself with the ancient clairvoyant forces, he might have found public recognition. Not only would people have cried Hosanna; they would have crowned him king. But a final pronouncement is made: Christ will form no link with the ancient forces. His sole aim is that humanity should find the way to awakening and freedom. It is no unloving curse that he utters on the fig trees of those who had lent him the ass and its colt. He acts purely from the nature of his own being. He is the sun, and when the sun rises, the moon perforce grows pale. So the moon-forces of the old vision fade away.

The Christ appears before the Temple. Many hundreds of pilgrims have assembled, and around the Temple buying and selling, trading and bargaining are being carried on. In the Temple itself a feverish activity prevails; sacrificial beasts are needed for the festival, the Passover lamb must be slaughtered. This is a source of business; for the animals have to be bought before they are sacrificed. Old Annas, the notorious miser of world history, knows how to make a profit. He has already made a vast fortune from this market. He has been the wire-puller in the political compromise with the Romans which is the basis of the Temple business. The pilgrims must change their local currency into the official currency which is valid in the Temple. This is Roman currency. Thus the Temple comprises also a Roman Exchange market. The Roman fiscal officers have been admitted to the Temple, although they were representatives of the cult of Caesar, because it was hoped by this compromise to keep them at least out of the Holy of Holies.

Now Christ comes on the scene. He is coming to fulfil the custom of the feast. But the fire of his burning will has its effect. There is no need for him to say much. The people are immediately seized with panic. Terror-stricken, they realize into what decadence they have fallen. Something similar had taken place at the feast of the Passover, three years before. At that time the terrifying effect came from the divine nature of the Christ, despite the conscious restraint which was still exercised by Jesus. But now the divinity is entirely transformed into humanity; it has become intensity of will. He has the right to tear down the mask of decadence of the Temple.

The sun of Christ shines, and the glimmer of the moon must fade away on the moon-hill of Mount Moriah. The spectres of the night flee from the sun. In place of a magnificent Temple appears a simple room on Mount Zion. There, in the Last Supper, the seed of a new ritual and worship, a sunlike sacrament, will be sown. The moon-religion of antiquity will be superseded on the evening of Maundy Thursday, when on the sun-hill of Mount Zion, Christ gives bread and wine to his disciples.

Luke 21:5–38

Apocalyptic words

[5]Some were speaking about the Temple, how beautifully adorned it was with precious stones and gift-offerings. [6]Then he said, 'You are only considering what you can see with eyes. But there will come times when not one stone will be left upon another; everything will become subject to destruction.'

[7]And they asked him, 'Master, when will this be? And by what sign shall we know that it is coming close?' [8]He said, 'Take care that no one leads you onto a wrong path. Many will come and, speaking in my name, will say: I am! and: The time has come! Do not follow them. [9]Then you will hear noise and tumult of war and revolution: Let it not give rise to fear in you. It is necessary for all this to happen. But the ultimate aim is yet far off.'

[10]And he went on: 'One part of humanity will rise against the other, and one kingdom against another. [11]There will be great earthquakes, epidemics and famines in many places; great and alarming phenomena will be seen in the sky. [12]But before this you will be seized and persecuted; you will be handed over to the teaching authorities and the prisons, and you will be dragged before kings and rulers for my name's sake. [13]Then it will be for you to bear witness. [14]But imprint it on your hearts that you shall not be anxious about how to defend yourselves. [15]From me you will receive both the words and the wisdom which none of your adversaries will be able to withstand or even contradict. [16]And you will also be betrayed by parents and brothers, relatives and friends. Some of you will be put to death, [17]and you will be hated by everyone for my name's sake. [18]But not a hair of your head shall be lost. [19]Through patient power of endurance you will then truly find yourselves.

[20]'So when you see Jerusalem surrounded by armies, then know that the time of its destruction has come. [21]Then all who

Tuesday in Holy Week

In the early morning Jesus enters the city with his disciples once more. The waves of acclamation and enthusiasm have long since died away. Jesus is already involved in the tension of his coming decision, but he will be obedient to the Law up to the last moment and fulfil the sacred customs of preparation for the Passover. There is the feeling that he himself is the sacrifice to be offered. The people's hatred is already surging up to him as flames that will consume the sacrifice. From day to day the powerful sense of his spiritual presence in the city has increased. The more silent the crowds, the more majestically his sovereign will shines in his countenance. Now the day of Mars has been reached and the conflict flares up in earnest. The crowd is silent; their leaders are full of anxiety; their fear produces the hatred which leads to the attack. Every hostile group sends out assailants. One after another they accost him with their crafty questions. What would otherwise be a blow in the face or a dagger-thrust takes on the guise of questioning.

First of all the members of the Jewish Sanhedrin approach: the high priests, scribes and elders. They ask Jesus what authority he has for his actions; He is required to legalize himself. Then come the others, the Pharisees and the Herodians, and put the insidious question: 'Is it lawful to give tribute unto Caesar?' The Sadducees follow. They ask Jesus' opinion concerning the resurrection of the dead. Finally, a single question, intending to expose him before all the people, asks are in Judea should flee to the mountains, and those who are in the town should leave, and those who are in the open country should not enter the town. ²²For then the days of higher justice have come, and everything written in the scriptures will be fulfilled. ²³Woe to those who are pregnant and the mothers who are breast-feeding when that time comes! For the distress of a grievous destiny is coming upon the earth, cosmic wrath will be discharged upon this people. ²⁴Many will fall by the edge of the sword and be dragged away into slavery among all the peoples of the world. And Jerusalem will be overrun and trampled upon by the heathen peoples until the time of the heathen peoples, too, is fulfilled.

²⁵'And signs will appear in sun, moon and stars, and there will be distress among the peoples of the earth and helplessness in the face of the surging sea and its mighty waves. ²⁶And human beings will lose their heads for fear and expectation of what is breaking in upon the whole earth. And even the forces of the heavens will be shaken. ²⁷Then the Son of Man will appear to seeing souls in the clouds of the sphere of life, borne up by the might of the World Powers, radiant with the glory of revelation. ²⁸And when all this begins to happen, straighten yourselves, stand upright and raise your heads, for then your redemption is drawing near.'

²⁹And he told them a parable: 'Look at the fig tree and all the other trees; ³⁰when they begin to come into leaf, you know from that that summer is near. ³¹So also, when you see all that begin to happen, you can know that the Kingdom of God is near. ³²Yes, I tell you, even before the time of people living now shall have come to an end, all that will begin to happen. ³³The heavens and the earth will pass away, but my words will not pass away.

³⁴'Take care that your hearts do not become unresponsive through dissipation and intoxication and the cares of material existence; otherwise the breaking of the Day will come upon you suddenly like a snare. ³⁵For that Day will come upon all who live on the earth. ³⁶So be of wakeful spirit at all times, school your souls in prayer, so that you may become strong to

which commandment he considers the most important of all.

These attacks, marking the outbreak of hostilities, are the best proof of how strongly the being of Christ was making itself felt. Just as dogs bark and bite only when they are afraid, so these ostensible questions, which are really arrows of hate, are the outcome of fear.

Jesus answers each of the four questions. He is not satisfied, however, with parrying the blows aimed at him; he accepts battle and fights back with weapons of the spirit. He uses powerful pictures. During the three previous years he has spoken to the people in poetic parables, and to the disciples in parables of deep mystery. To his opponents he now speaks parables of conflict. He tells the parable of the husbandmen to whom the vineyard has been entrusted; how they afterwards refuse to surrender the harvest, slay the owner's messengers, and finally even his son. The opponents realize that they themselves are meant. In fact, Jesus is telling his enemies that they will slay him. His parable is a last endeavour to reach the souls of his enemies. Perhaps it may yet bring them to an awakening; perhaps even now they may be shocked into self-knowledge.

The parable of the royal marriage feast follows. Guests are called to the marriage, and they all excuse themselves from attending. Then the invitation is passed on to strangers, to people who seem to have no occasion for coming. Because the duly licensed and established seekers after God have proved to be

live through all that is coming without being harmed, and to
be able to stand before the revelation of the Son of Man.'

[37]He spent the days teaching in the Temple, but at night he
left the town and stayed on the Mount of Olives. [38]And already
early in the morning all the people flocked to him to hear him
in the Temple.

hypocrites, God finally summons people whom one would not credit with seeking the divine. This is a direct thrust at his opponents, who are the privileged religious people by ancient tradition. But when the fate of those wearing no wedding garment is described, a stern mirror is held up before the whole of humanity. The parable of the king's marriage feast is the strongest thrust dealt on the Mars day of Passion Week, directed ultimately to all people.

The Christ goes further; he now questions back. 'Whose son is the Messiah?' he asks. They answer: 'The son of David.' Christ cites the words of Psalm 110, well known to them, to show that David describes the Messiah as his Lord. He asks: 'How then can David, inspired by the Spirit, call him his Lord ... Since David calls him his Lord, how then can he be his son?' Christ exposes the superficial piety of his questioners; they are looking only at the earthly. The first step towards grasping the divine is to see that the Messiah is a Son of God and not a son of men. Christ is showing them at this moment what they should recognize in him, but they do not recognize it.

And so it comes to the fourth counterblow. This is the ninefold woe, the denunciation of the Pharisees which is followed by the lament over Jerusalem, as over a world doomed to destruction. At the beginning of his work, in the trusted circle of the disciples, Jesus once pronounced the nine beatitudes in the Sermon on the Mount, the ninefold ideal of Spirit Man. Now at the close of his earthly path he sets the ninefold shadow over against the ninefold light. The denunciations

are a combative unmasking of those who are inimi-
cal to God, just as the beatitudes were a revelation
of man's ninefold relation to God. In the lamentation
over Jerusalem there is the reverse of the promise of
the 'city set upon a hill,' which in the Sermon on the
Mount calls up for the first time the picture of the
heavenly Jerusalem.

As the day begins to decline, Jesus leaves the city
with his disciples, as was his custom. He climbs the
hill of Gethsemane beyond the vale of Kidron, and
enters the garden which had been the scene of so much
intimate teaching; but he does not continue towards
Bethphage and Bethany. At the top of the Mount of
Olives, where a wonderful peace surrounds them, he
makes the disciples rest. Still imbued with the conflict
which has been waged all day, he begins to speak to
his disciples in the open air for the last time. And the
words with which he instructs them are no less powerful than those he has spoken in the spiritual fight with
his opponents. The courageous deeds which have been
accomplished by the soul during the day call up an
echo from the gods. The Christ can make revelations
to his disciples as never before. What he gives on this
evening, sometimes known as the Little Apocalypse,
opens vast horizons of the future.

So it is always in life. If real deeds have ripened
during the day, then evening and night call down a
heavenly echo. The results of a day do not only lie in
what has been directly achieved. When the activities
of the day have knocked on the doors of the spiritual
world, then with night descending the gates of another

world can open. Genuine inner strength employed during the day is met by a spiritual response.

The present moment becomes translucent. All through the day the disciples have been with Christ near the Temple. He has shown them that it is all doomed to destruction. The destruction of Jerusalem and the Temple was a spiritual necessity and if it had not come to pass four decades later through the Roman army, it would have had to be brought about in some other way. As the vision of the downfall of the Temple rises before the disciples, a great cosmic catastrophe seems to shine through it. It is the downfall of a whole world that the Christ sets before their souls. The division, manifest all day between the hostile opponents and the little band striving for discipleship — this too becomes translucent. The history of the world will bring nothing less than a great dividing of humankind. Some strive towards the divine; others strive against it. And no matter how imposing what is accomplished on earth by the antagonists, it is only the outcome of a hidden fear. That which silently germinates in the little group seeking union with the divine will bear in itself the future of the world.

Jesus continues the apocalyptic discourse, and gives the disciples the most intimate parables that he can possibly give them, the two parables of the Second Coming. He had already spoken of the Son of Man coming in the clouds, while all around the universal storm is raging. He had pointed to a future where a new revelation of Christ must force a way for itself amidst hurricanes of destruction. Now, in

the two parables of the ten virgins and the talents, he
shows the disciples what people must do to prepare
themselves for the return of the Christ. Some day the
bridegroom of the soul will come; some day the one
who entrusted the talents to his servants when he went
away, will come again to claim the reckoning. Down
below in the Temple the 'woe,' 'woe,' sounded as anti-
beatitudes; now the day ends with another Sermon
on the Mount, one even more sublime. With this final
and most intimate teaching Christ arms the disciples
with equipment of courage for millennia ahead. The
parables of the Second Coming, and in particular the
concluding vision of the division of humanity into
sheep and goats, are to serve the disciples as provision
on the road for many incarnations.

The words of the Tuesday in Holy Week, taken
together, are wonderfully relevant to every battle of
light with darkness, every struggle for Christian discipleship in conflict with Christ's enemies. Goethe's
statement that world history is nothing but a continuous fight of belief against unbelief touches the truth that
is given in all detail during the Tuesday of Holy Week.
All opposition to Christ and hostility to the spirit has its
root in unbelief, in deeply hidden weakness and fear.
Discipleship of Christ means courage and strength. The
battle is not necessarily fought by one group of men
against another. It must be carried on within ourselves.
In each human soul fear and courage, opposition to
Christ and discipleship of Christ, are mingled.

The fighting parables directed against Christ's
opponents make it clear that fear is always at the root

of enmity to the spirit. The egotism of the husbandmen of the vineyard, who are unwilling to surrender the fruits of the harvest, is the offspring of inner weakness and fear — as is every egotism. When a man learns to leave and sacrifice all because he realizes that all he can ever possess is the property of God, the first seed of courage is born.

The denunciations uttered by Christ are an ever plainer unmasking of unbelief. They begin at once with words which tear away the mask not only of denial of the spirit, but of every kind of dragooning of human souls: 'Woe to you, scribes and Pharisees, you hypocrites! You shut the kingdom of the heavens against men. You cannot find entrance yourselves, and so you want to bar the entrance to those who can find it.' (Matt.23:13).

To work upon one's own soul demands the greatest courage. The wedding garment is the soul become radiant through purification and prayer. The oil in the lamps is a picture of the forces of the soul to be won by struggle. The talents increased by personal effort are the spiritual organs in man brought to further development.

In his answer concerning the tribute money Jesus shows that true courage attained through constant inner effort is able to hold the balance between earthly duties and spiritual ideals, and in so doing gains sovereignty over all earthly conditions. Even if, as at that time, a monster occupies the throne, he is able to say 'Render unto Caesar the things which are Caesar's and unto God the things which are God's.'

In the concluding vision of the dividing of humanity, the true quality of inner courage is described: 'Yes,
I say to you, what you did for the least of my brothers,
that you did for me.' The true path to the spirit shows
itself in the power to love. Love is the opposite of fear.
All genuine inner development begins with inner
courage and finds its goal in love. True love of men is
identical with love for Christ himself, so his words of
spiritual battle end in words of love.

Matthew 26:3–16

Anointing in Bethany
³And the chief priests and the elders of the people gathered in the hall of the high priest Caiaphas ⁴and made a resolution to get Jesus into their power by treachery and to kill him. ⁵They said to themselves, however: It had best not be during the festival, in case there should be an uprising among the people.

⁶When Jesus was in Bethany in the house of Simon the leper, ⁷a woman came up to him with an alabaster jar of the most precious ointment; and she poured it on his head as he sat at table. ⁸When the disciples saw it, they were indignant and said, 'Why this waste? ⁹It could have been sold for a large sum and the proceeds given to the poor.' ¹⁰But Jesus perceived their thoughts and said, 'Why do you plague the woman? She has done a good deed to me. ¹¹The poor you will always have with you, but you will not always have me. ¹²By anointing my body she has prepared me for burial. ¹³Yes, I say to you, wherever in the whole world this Gospel is proclaimed, what she has done will be told and her memory will be honoured.'

Betrayal by Judas
¹⁴Then one of the twelve, Judas Iscariot, went to the chief priests ¹⁵and said, 'What will you give me if I deliver him into your hands?' And they offered him thirty pieces of silver. ¹⁶From then on he sought an opportunity to betray him.

Wednesday in Holy Week

The 'Still Week' — as Holy Week is called in some countries — is not really still until the middle day is past. On Palm Sunday the city was in a state of tremor; on Monday the tables of the vendors and money-changers were overturned in the Temple; on Tuesday, sword-thrusts were dealt in spiritual conflict between Christ and his opponents. It is not until the last part of the week that stillness descends. Wednesday, Mercury's day, is the turning point. The mercurial element of living movement, represents the transition from the first unquiet days of the 'Still Week' to those in which the consummation of Christ's life moves into ever deeper stillness.

Towards evening on Wednesday a scene stands out which, although it has also occurred before, takes on a special significance on this middle day of balance. Christ has turned from the tumult of the city to the quiet country town of Bethany, beyond the Mount of Olives. He stays in the circle of those with whom he is particularly united. A meal has been prepared for him as on other evenings. But it is as though a certain radiance fell upon the scene, shining in advance from the meal which will be celebrated the next day. A presentiment of the Last Supper hovers round the community at table. The country town of Bethany, quiet as it is, has shortly before been the scene of the raising of Lazarus, the event which had given the signal for battle. Lazarus is one of those gathered round the table; and it is he, as we know, who is described by the gospel as resting on the heart of Jesus the next evening. At the Last Supper it is he who is nearest to Christ, both outwardly and inwardly.

Two women also belong to the community at table, Martha and Mary Magdalene, whom the Gospel of John states to be the sisters of Lazarus. They have been led by the hand of providence into this circle, which is more related by the spirit than by blood. In the life of each of these three persons there has been an event which brought a radical transformation. For Lazarus it was the awakening from the grave, the great release of the John-spirit for its flight to the heights. For Mary Magdalene the event lay somewhat farther back; it is called in the gospel a 'driving out of devils.' She had been healed of the tragedy of 'possession' and had experienced the freeing and purifying of her soul. For Martha there had also been a significant event; she is said in early Christian tradition to be the woman who was healed of the issue of blood. Destiny had decreed that she should bring with her into life a weakness through which her bodily organism was unable to hold its forces together. Through meeting with the one who could heal her, a staying power, a formative force, drew into her body, just as an inner peace had entered the soul of Mary Magdalene. The brother and sisters of Bethany became the intimate friends of Christ through healings of the spirit, the soul and the body.

As they all sit at table with the disciples, Mary is recorded as having anointed the feet of Christ with precious pure nard ointment and wiped them with her hair. John's Gospel says that the whole house was filled with the perfume. Mary Magdalene had performed a similar act a year and a half previously. She had experienced a freeing and redeeming through her meeting with the Christ, and in order to show her overflowing gratitude she had, as the Gospel of Luke describes, anointed the feet of Christ and dried them with her hair. John's Gospel, in the introductory words to the awakening of Lazarus, refers to this earlier scene (11:2). Mary Magdalene is described in St Luke's Gospel as the 'great sinner,' and it is possible, according to old traditions, that she was a prostitute, driven by demons, in the worldly spa town of Tiberias, near her home at Magdala. But what does her act of anointing signify now? It is the type and symbol of a sacramental act. Therefore, when others declare her deed extravagant and become indignant, Christ can accept what this woman does as a sacrament of death, as a fulfilment of the Last Anointing. On the occasion of the earlier anointing he had said, 'Her many sins are forgiven her, for she has shown much love.' And one can feel how Mary has since been able to deepen the natural forces of earthly love erring on false paths, and transmute them into religious devotion, and the capacity for sacrifice.

Then the solemn stillness is suddenly broken by a figure who forms a complete contrast to Mary Magdalene. It is one of the apostles, and as he sees the deed of Mary he loses all self-control. This is Judas. He says that the precious money which has just been squandered could have been given to the poor, and thus many social needs might have been relieved.

John's Gospel, however, makes it plain that his real
motives are not the ostensible ones. The gospel openly
calls him a thief. It may well be that the anger which
Judas felt at the deed of Mary Magdalene gave the
final impetus to his act of betrayal. He had waited a
long time in tense expectation that Jesus would come
forward publicly: then a political miracle would inevi-
tably follow. In his feverish impatience, it seems to him
that Christ wastes his time; and finally at Bethany his
patience can endure no more. In uncontrolled irrita-
tion he goes out to those who lie in wait for the Christ.
The second crucial event of the Wednesday is the
betrayal by Judas.

Both Judas and Mary Magdalene are typical
Mercury people; they are active and temperamental.
One of the virtues of their nature is that they are never
tedious; something is always happening round them.
Mary Magdalene, however, subdues her restlessness
and transforms it into devotion, peace and the capacity for love. One can see from the gospel account that
true devotion is the final achievement of an active soul,
a soul for whom peace is not mere immobility, but
mobility redeemed, made inward. Mary Magdalene
has been storm-tossed; she has endured sinister experiences. But now an intense power of devotion grows
from all that was formerly dark and disturbing. This
intensity will later lift her above all other human
beings; to her it is granted to be the first to meet and
behold the Risen Christ.

Judas is the type of the restless man who must
always be outwardly active. He pretends to want

something for the poor. However good and com-
mendable social activity may be, it is often only self-
deception. The underlying motive is not always a
genuine social impulse, but very often one's own inner
restlessness. Many people would be most unhappy if
they were obliged to do nothing for a time. It would
then be seen that their social zeal is no true inner activity, but a yielding to an unacknowledged weakness.
In Judas this kind of mercurial soul meets with a dark
fate. His unrest springs from a deeply hidden fear, and
it leads to his betrayal of Christ Jesus. Such a soul cannot show devotion; above all, it cannot love. A restless
person is not capable of real love; for love is possible
only where the soul has found peace. Thus in the two
figures, Mary Magdalene and Judas, two roads separate, as at a crossroads. One leads to the realization of
the nearness of Christ; the other into dark night, into
the tragedy of suicide.

Martha, the other sister of Lazarus, is a transition,
as it were, between Judas and Mary Magdalene. Luke's
Gospel tells the story of Mary and Martha earlier on,
and has a purpose in doing so. Martha is the constantly
active one who cannot exist without undertaking some
service. One cannot deny the genuine nature of her
devotion, but one must not be blind to the fact that
the unrest from which she was healed in the body has
remained in her soul. Mary, who listens with devotion,
is described as the one who has chosen the good part.

The figures taking part in these scenes on the
Wednesday show us the crossroads which we must
face before we may hope for admittance to the sphere

of Maundy Thursday. The ways separate in face of the
mystery of the sacrament. Judas is the man without
ritual. He becomes restless and loses self-control when
he comes into the sphere of true ceremonial worship.
Mary Magdalene is the sacramental soul. On the following evening, when the circle of disciples will be
united in the sacrament as under a great dome, it will
be apparent who is nearer to Mary, and who to Judas.

Mercury, who for the Greco-Roman world was
both the god of healing and also the god of merchants
and of thieves, comes now into the orbit of the Christ-
sun. The scene in the house of Lazarus and her sisters
at Bethany shows how Mercury, the god of healing,
can himself be healed by the sun of Christ.

Matthew 26:17–29

The Last Supper

[17]On the first day of the Unleavened Bread the disciples came to Jesus and said, 'Where do you want us to prepare the Passover meal?' [18]He said, 'Go into the town, you know to whom, and say to him, "The Master says: My time is near. With you will I celebrate the Passover festival with my disciples".' [19]And the disciples carried out the directions Jesus had given them, and they prepared the Passover meal.

[20]And in the evening he sat down to the meal with the twelve disciples. [21]And while they were eating he said, 'Yes, I tell you, one of you will betray me.' [22]Then they became very sad and asked him one after another, 'Is it I, Lord?' [23]He answered, 'He who dips the bread with me in the dish will betray me. [24]The Son of Man must die, as the scriptures also say about him. But woe to that man by whom the Son of Man is betrayed! For that man it would be better if he had never been born.' [25]Then said Judas who betrayed him, 'Is it I, Master?' And Jesus said, 'You said it.'

[26]And while they were eating, Jesus took the bread, blessed it, broke it and gave it to the disciples and said, 'Take and eat, this is my body.' [27]And he took the cup, blessed it and gave it to the disciples and said, 'Drink of it, all of you, [28]for this is the blood of the covenant; it is shed for many for the overcoming of the sickness of sin. [29]And I say to you: From now on I will no longer drink of this gift of the vine until the day when I, in renewed form, drink it with you in the realm of my Father.'

Maundy Thursday

On Maundy Thursday evening a holy stillness descends, and all the clamour of the first half of the week passes into silence. By day the sounds of swarming streets, the bargaining and noisy talking of thousands of Passover pilgrims, have reached their peak. Then, shortly before the deep red sun has sunk in the west, faced by the silver disc of the rising full moon, the trumpets sound from the Temple and give the signal for the beginning of the day of preparation. On the eve of the Passover, the faithful of the old covenant are preparing for the Sabbath, which begins on the following evening. In every house people gather round the table to eat the Passover lamb in the circle of their blood-relations. The streets are suddenly emptied and an oppressive silence falls. It is the curfew of Passover night, when the destroying angel is abroad, as once long ago, in Egypt.

So Jesus and his disciples also withdraw to the room in which they are to celebrate the Passover. The stillness of this room is enhanced, for providence has brought them to no private dwelling, but to the house of the order of the Essenes. The Cenacle, which the Essene brotherhood has placed at the service of Jesus and his disciples for the eve of the Passover, stands on holy ground. Here, on Mount Zion, a sanctuary of humanity has existed from times immemorial. Immediately opposite, also on a traditional spot, stands the house of Caiaphas, the ancestral home of the Sadducean order. A circle has gathered there

John 17

The High Priestly prayer
When he had said this, Jesus raised his vision to the spirit
and said, 'Father, the hour has come; reveal the being of your
Son, so that your Son may reveal your being. [2]You have made
him the creating power in all earthly human bodies, that he
may give true life to all who came to him through you. [3]And
the true life is this, that they recognize you as the one true
Ground of the World, and Jesus Christ as the one whom you
have sent to them. [4]I have revealed your being on the earth and
have fulfilled the task which you have given me to do. [5]And
now, Father, Ground of the World, let my being be revealed in
the light which shone about me in your presence, before the
world yet was. [6]I have made manifest your name to those human beings who have come out of the world to me through
you. Yours they were, and you have given them to me, and they
have kept your word in their inmost being. [7]Thus they have
recognized that everything which you have given me is from
you; [8]for all the power of the word which you have given me, I
have brought to them. They have taken it into themselves and
have recognized in deepest truth that I come from you, and
they have come to believe that I have been sent by you. [9]I pray
to you for them as individual human beings, not for mankind
in general. Only for the human beings which you have given
me, because they belong to you. [10]Everything that is mine is
yours, and what is yours is mine, and the light of my being can
shine in them. [11]I am now no longer in the world of the senses;
but they are still in the world of the senses. And I am coming
to you. Holy Father, keep, through the power of your being,
those who came to me through you, so that they may become
one, as we are one. [12]As long as I have been with them, I have
kept and sheltered, through the power of your being, those
who came to me through you, and none of them has been lost
except he who was born to be an instrument of destruction;

also to celebrate the Passover. They can scarcely give thought to the coming feast, for they are actively concerned with a plan of hatred and enmity. For a time the struggle must cease; the holy hour must first have passed. And so his enemies themselves give the order — 'Seek to arrest him, but not at the Feast.' In the room where Jesus is assembled with his disciples, the words of Psalm 23 are fulfilled: 'Thou preparest a table before me in the presence of my enemies.'

The Passover lamb on the table in the Cenacle assumes a new meaning. At the table is seated the one of whom John the Baptist could say: 'See, the Lamb of God, who takes the sin of the world upon himself' (John 1:29). Nowhere in that hour nor ever before nor since, has the Passover lamb been so near to the one for whom it was an image. For thousands of years the eating of the Passover lamb was a prophetic custom, and now the fulfilment of the prophecy is at hand. The apostle Paul will presently be able to say, 'Our passover lamb has been killed: that is Christ' (1Cor.5:7). In the Cenacle, prophecy and fulfilment meet each other. A heavy foreboding fills the room; separation and tragedy rest in the air. Christ's death of sacrifice throws its shadow before and the consciousness of the disciples has a heavy test to endure.

The ancient tradition of blood-sacrifice has its symbol in the Passover lamb upon the table. The magic of the blood, signified by all pre-Christian blood-sacrifices, has an active power. It was believed that the shedding of the blood of pure sacrificial animals was able to transport people's souls, formerly more loosely and so scripture has been fulfilled. [13]Now I am coming to you, and I am saying these words while I am still among human-kind, so that my joy may be fulfilled in them. [14]I have brought them your word; but other people have hated them because they are not of their world, as I, also, am not of their world. [15]My prayer is not that you should take them out of the earthly world, but that you protect them from the evil. [16]They are not of the earthly world, as I, also, am not of that world. [17]Hallow them through the truth. Your word is Truth. [18]As you sent me into the world, so now I have sent them into the world. [19]And I consecrate myself for them, so that they may be consecrated in truth. [20]And not only for them do I pray to you, but also for those who will unite with me through their proclamation, [21]so that they may all be one; as you, Father, are in me and I in you, so they shall be one in us, so that the world may come to believe that you have sent me. [22]I have given them the power of revelation which you have given me, so that they may be one, as we are one. [23]I am in them, and you are in me, and so they are consecrated to become perfectly one, so that the world may recognize that you have sent me and that you love them as you love me.

[24]'Father, Ground of the World, that is my will: That those whom you have given me may ever be with me where I am and that there they will behold the revelation of my being which you, in your love, have given me before the world was. [25]Exalt-ed Father, earthly human beings have not recognized you; but I have recognized you, and these have recognized that you sent me. [26]I have revealed your name to them, and I will continue to reveal it, so that the love with which you have loved me may remain in them and so my being may be revealed in them.'

united with the body, into a state of ecstasy. Divine
forces from the other world could then be reflected in
human conditions. And now the ancient sacrifice loses
its significance for ever in the Cenacle on Mount Zion.
The divine being has now himself entered this world;
therefore the old blood-sacrifice has become superflu-
ous. The power which it was sought formerly to bring
down from other worlds is now there, come to unite
itself inseparably with this world. The Passover lamb
has magical forces no longer, for in earth-existence
itself a seed of heavenly forces is being formed. The
lamb becomes the pure image of the sacrificial deed of
divine love.

On the table of the holy meal, however, there is also
bread and wine. And when the ancient custom of the
Passover meal has been observed, Christ takes, to the
astonishment of the disciples, these other representatives of food and drink and adds a new meal to that
ordained by the Old Testament. It is a new and unexpected deed when Christ gives to his disciples bread
and wine and says: 'Take, this is my body — this is
my blood.' But these symbols are not on the table by
accident. Something comes to light which has always
existed. Externally blood-sacrifices were carried out in
the Temple in the presence of the people, but in hidden
sanctuaries esoteric sun-mysteries had always been
preserved, where bread and wine were the symbols
of the sun god. On the very spot where now the circle
were gathered at the Last Supper, the sanctuary of
Melchizedek had stood, whence he took forth bread
and wine and carried them down to the valley of

Kidron to dispense them to Abraham. Now bread and
wine became more than symbols. The divine sun-spirit
is present in Christ, and as he distributes the bread he
can say: 'This is my body,' and in handing the disciples
the chalice: 'This is my blood.' His soul surrenders
itself and streams into the bread and wine. In the twilight of the room bread and wine are enveloped with a
shining sun-aura. Inasmuch as they become body and
blood of the Christ soul, they become body and blood
of the sun-spirit himself. All the sun-mysteries of antiquity were but prophecy; at this moment they grow into
fulfilment. In the transition from the blood offerings of
the past to the bloodless offering of bread and wine,
the whole idea of sacrifice changed. Ancient sacrifices
were always material offerings. Now the sacrifice of
the soul is founded, and there begins the true tradition
of inner sacrifice. The lunar sacrifices of antiquity are
at an end; the solar sacrifice of Christianity comes into
being. Christianity, the true sun religion, dawns in this
evening hour.

By performing significant acts before and after the
meal, Christ brings about a fourfold whole, anticipat-
ing the four parts of the central Christian sacrament
which thenceforward will be continually celebrated.
Before the meal he follows the custom observed in the
order of the Essenes and washes the feet of each of
the disciples, even of Judas. A deeply moving picture,
unfathomable in its full significance: Christ utterly
surrendering himself in loving devotion, on which his
death will soon set the seal. After the meal another
ceremonial act is observed by Christ, this time in

accord with the custom followed by all the neighbour-
ing households at this hour. When the Passover has
been eaten, the head of the family begins to recite from
the Haggada, the history of the people from ancient
times set down in legendary form. With Christ, too,
the meal is followed by a discourse. This is recorded
and gathered together by St John in the wonderful
Farewell Discourse culminating in the High Priestly
Prayer (John 17).

Four stages are passed through: the washing of the
feet, the Passover lamb, the bread and wine, and the
Farewell Discourse. The washing of the feet sums up
in a pictorial act the essence of Christ's teaching: 'This
is the task I put before you, that you love one another'
(15:12). The washing of the feet is, as it were, the last
of the parables, enacted, not merely spoken. It teaches
love as the ultimate purpose of Christ's gospel. The eating of the Passover lamb corresponds in the structure
of the communion service to the stage of the Offering,
which follows the Reading of the Gospel. The image
of the Offering emerges: Christ the Passover Lamb
who on the next day dies for humanity on the cross.
Then comes the third stage: Christ gives the disciples
bread and wine. For the first time Transubstantiation
is consummated, forming the third part of the sacrament, after the Reading of the Gospel and the Offering.
Now the spiritual lights up in earthly substance. In the
Farewell Discourse, the fourth stage, Christ imparts to
the disciples the most intimate information about his
own being. These words are body and blood of Christ in
a still higher degree than the bread and wine. The soul

of Christ gives itself to the souls of the disciples who are only able to receive them as yet as though in a dream. Only John, who lies at the breast of Jesus, and listens to the speaking heart of Christ, is able in his gospel to preserve for humanity a reflection of this moment.

Christ, from whom proceeds the stream of cosmic love, speaks at the same time as the spirit of wisdom. It is as though Jupiter, the god of wisdom, has appeared in new form among men.

The sacred Round Table breaks up dramatically. It is a strict regulation of the Passover that on this night no one may leave the protection of the house. If he does so, he meets the destroying angel. The streets remain empty of people. In spite of this, at a certain moment, someone does go out; he does not delay after he has received the bread from Jesus' hand. St John's Gospel adds: 'It was night.' It was also night within Judas; at this moment Satan entered into him. Judas goes to the house opposite, where Caiaphas and his circle are keeping the Passover. They are ready and eager for the business that Judas wants to transact.

The soul of Judas founders on the mystery of the sacrament. On the evening before, as the sacramental mood unfolded in the house at Bethany, he was already seized with the demon of unrest. In the Cenacle he has met the sacramental substance for the second time. Peace within himself would alone enable him to receive the blessing of peace through the sacrament, but this he does not possess. So that which could dispense peace to him serves to throw him into the final restlessness, into the Ahrimanic displacing of the ego, and possession.

Once more the Passover is broken. Jesus rises from the table and beckons to the astonished disciples. They follow him out into the night, where the light of the full moon had for some time been almost extinguished. It is passing through an eclipse. The frosty chills of winter giving place to spring begin to be felt as Jesus goes with his disciples to Gethsemane.

The two acts of going-out-into-the-night symbolize inner events. The going out of Judas shows that his true self has abandoned him; outside he meets the angel of death in reality. Ahrimanic spirits make him their pawn. The going-out of Christ is a picture of the free surrender of the soul which has been from the beginning the cosmic bearer of sacrifice. As Judas goes out, the gospel says, 'It was night' and the soul of Judas is also shrouded in night. As the Christ goes out, one could say, 'It was day.' A golden shimmer mingles with the chilly night as the Christ goes down with the disciples the same path into the valley that was trodden two thousand years before by Melchizedek, carrying down bread and wine.

The shining aura which people saw radiating from the being of Christ on Palm Sunday has now contracted into much deeper levels. No one perceives it, yet the world receives a new glory on this holy evening, which is more an Easter Eve than an eve of Good Friday. On that other Thursday, Ascension day six weeks later, the seed of light, whose growth began in the Cenacle, will have already spread over the whole earth with cosmic power.

John 19:1–27

Crowning with thorns

Then Pilate took Jesus and had him scourged. [2]And the soldiers plaited a crown of thorns and put it on his head and threw a purple cloak round him, [3]walked up to him and said, 'Hail, King of the Jews!' And they struck him in the face. [4]And again Pilate went out and said to them, 'See, thus I bring him out to you, so that you may know that I find no guilt in him.' [5]And Jesus came out, wearing the crown of thorns and the purple cloak. And he said to them, 'See, this is Man.' [6]When the chief priests and the Temple attendants saw him, they shouted: 'Crucify, crucify him!' Then Pilate said to them, 'Take him yourselves and crucify him, for I find no guilt in him.' [7]Then the Jews replied, 'We have a law, and according to that law he must die, because he has made himself a Son of God.'

The judgment

[8]When Pilate heard these words, he was even more alarmed, [9]and he again went into the courthouse and said to Jesus, 'From where have you received your mission?' But Jesus gave him no answer. [10]Then Pilate said to him, 'You will not speak to me? Do you not know that I have the power to release you and also to crucify you?' [11]Jesus answered, 'You would not have power over me unless it had been given you from on high. Therefore the greater burden of destiny falls upon him who handed me over to you.' [12]Upon this, Pilate wanted to set him free. But the Jews shouted: 'If you release him, you are no longer a friend of Caesar; for everyone who makes himself a king is against Caesar.' [13]When he had heard these words, Pilate led Jesus out and sat down on the judgment seat in the place called The Pavement; in Hebrew, Gabbatha. [14]It was the Day of Preparation of the Passover festival, about midday. And he said to the Jews, 'See, this is your King.' [15]But they shouted: 'Away with him, away with him,

Good Friday

As the still week really enters into stillness, the bearing of Jesus changes. His fiery fighting will is no longer evident. When between midnight and sunrise the band of soldiers lays hand upon him whom Judas has kissed, he does not oppose them. Rather, he opposes Peter who wants to fight for him. Then he is seized by rough hands and dragged through the city, from one end to the other. He is apparently delivered, helpless, to those who scourge him, press the crown of thorns on his brow, spit upon him and strike him in the face. The witnesses of the tragedy are overcome with anguish as he who has no physical strength left is forced to carry the heavy cross and is nailed upon it by the executioners with pitiless cruelty. What has become of the fighting power which blazed in him during the first days of the week? Has he abandoned the battle against the blindness and wickedness of men? No, the fight which was waged on the human level on the previous days is now carried on in a higher sphere, and so takes on still more powerful dimensions. Christ is not fighting against flesh and blood, but against the invisible demonic powers from whose tyranny he will deliver humanity. He fights against the Luciferic powers, the glittering beings of deceptive light, who want to estrange man from the earth and, likewise, against the Ahrimanic powers who want to harden and fetter man to dead matter. As Christ seems to lay down the weapons, he is really following the satanic powers into their hiding-places in order to overcome them there.

crucify him!' Pilate asked them, 'Shall I crucify your King?' And
the chief priests answered, 'We have no king but Caesar.' ¹⁶Then
he handed him over to them to be crucified.

The Crucifixion

¹⁷And they seized Jesus and, carrying his own the cross, he
went out to the Place of a Skull, in Hebrew called Golgotha.
¹⁸There they crucified him, and with him two others, one on
the one side, the other on the other side, and Jesus in the middle. ¹⁹Pilate had written a title and fixed it on the cross. It read:
JESUS OF NAZARETH, THE KING OF THE JEWS. ²⁰This title was
read by many Jews, for the place where Jesus was crucified was
near the city. It was written in Hebrew, in Latin and in Greek.
²¹Then the chief priests of the Jews said to Pilate, 'Do not write:
"The King of the Jews," but "This man said: I am the King of
the Jews"'. ²²But Pilate answered, 'What I have written I have
written.'

²³Now when the soldiers had crucified Jesus they took his
garments and divided them into four parts, one for each sol-
dier. Then they also took the cloak. This cloak was seamless,
woven in one piece from top to bottom. ²⁴Then they said to
one another, 'Let us not tear it, but cast lots to see whose it
shall be.' The word of scripture was to be fulfilled:

They divided my clothes among them,
      and for my cloak they cast lots.
²⁵Therefore the soldiers did this.

Standing by the cross of Jesus were his mother and his
mother's sister, Mary the wife of Clopas, and Mary of Magdala.
²⁶Now when Jesus saw his mother standing there and the disciple whom he loved, he said to his mother, 'Woman, see, that
is your son.' ²⁷And then he said to the disciple, 'See, that is your
mother.' And from that hour the disciple took her to himself.

Ahriman displays his power over people most tri-
umphantly when he approaches in the form of death.
In humanity's evolution up to the 'turning-point of
time,' death which had formerly been a friend of man
had taken on more and more the features of Ahriman.
The dark power knew how to use man's destiny of
death to make it his sharpest weapon. The power of
death is not only that we must die; it becomes really
manifest only after death. When we have laid aside
our earthly body it must then be proved whether we
can still maintain a connection with what takes place
on earth among those to whom we belong. Here lies
death's actual power — that it can wrest us from
earthly things and thrust us out into the unbridgeable
exile of life on the other side. The Ahrimanic power of
death uses the earth to mock at man. During earthly
life it binds him to the world of matter; it makes all
sorts of promises of earthly fulfilment, which are no
longer kept after death. The more a man is attached to
the things of 'this side' during life, the more inexorably
he is affected by 'other-sidedness' after death. Only
those people who have gained a firm foothold in the
life of the spirit during life on earth can after death
remain helpfully united with those who are still living
on earth. After death we have only as much spiritual
command over matter as we have gained upon earth.

When on Maundy Thursday Christ dispenses the
Last Supper to the disciples in the peace of the
Cenacle, there seems to be no conflict. And yet what
a wonderful victory over the spirit of dead matter is
shown when the Christ takes in his hand the earthly

substances of bread and wine, and makes them lumi-
nous through the sun-force of his heart. He wrests the
terrestrial creature from the powers of darkness and
makes it the body and blood of his being of light. As
he is able during his life to ensoul the earthly elements
so that these become radiant, he will have all the more
power to do so after death.

In Gethsemane the fight against the power of death
enters a decisive phase. Here in the quiet grove of the
Mount of Olives, where he has so often been with his
disciples for intimate teaching, he must now withstand
the most dangerous attack of the enemy in utmost
loneliness.* The community which he has just established in the upper room for the future wellbeing of
humanity does not bring help and benefit to himself.
The consciousness of the disciples has not grown to
the greatness of the moment. Judas has gone out into
the night of betrayal, but the others, too, leave their
Master in the lurch. They are absorbed in the twilight
of their sleep in Gethsemane, out of which Peter will
deny Christ.

It is not inner weakness and fear of death with
which Christ has to wrestle in Gethsemane. One
could not misunderstand more tragically the whole
Passion of Christ than by thinking that Jesus prayed in
Gethsemane that he might still be spared from death.
Not fear of death, but death itself assails him. Death,
already apprehensive of losing control over him,
appears before him to lay hold of him. The destroying
angel wants to possess him. The secret of the conflict in
Gethsemane lies in the fact that death wants to outwit

Jesus. It wants to wrest him away too soon, before he has ended his work and filled the last vestige of the earthly vessel with his spirit.

For three years the fire of divine egohood has burned in the body and soul of Jesus. The human vessel — from within outwards — has thus already been consumed almost to ashes. What still has to be suffered and completed demands so much strength from the earthly sheaths that there is a real danger of premature death. Ahriman lies in wait and hopes to make use of this moment. Luke, the physician, describes with precise words what happens, when he says 'And as he was in the throes of death he prayed with even greater intensity.' In the clinical sense of the term, the death-struggle had already come. When Luke adds, 'and his sweat became as drops of blood which fell to the earth,' he adds exact symptoms of the agony of death (Luke 22:44).

But Christ is victorious and death is repulsed. With the mightiest force of prayer ever known on earth he wrestles to remain in the body. It is an echo of this fight when he speaks on the cross the words that seem to betray a weakness: 'I thirst.' He still remains, even immediately before he breathes out his soul, true to the earth. It is not his will to pass into the spiritual world simply through dying. It is his will to remain united with the earth when he goes through death, and it is this that is to be his conquest over death. He wrestles to enter still more deeply into the earthly world of matter which he bears in himself through his physical body. There is still a last remnant to be ensouled. This, too, he will not abandon to the Prince of this World, who has begun to count on the material realm of the earthly as being in his possession once and for all.

The drama returns to human scenes and conditions. On the morning of Good Friday Christ confronts the whole of humanity, as represented by the three figures of Caiaphas, Pilate and Herod. Then the way leads up to Golgotha. Nails are driven by the soldiers into the hands and feet of the Christ, and it seems as though he allows everything to come about quite passively. In fact, through the medicine of bitter pain, his inmost being has gained the ultimate power of spirit over matter, so that death can no longer claim him. The Ahrimanic death-powers realize this, and appear for their last effort, furious that their might has been of no avail. When the sun is darkened during the sultry midday hours of Good Friday, it is as though the demon of the sun were straining to the utmost against the god of the sun. And when the earth is shaken by the earthquake, all the demons of the earth seem to storm forward in an endeavour to help the satanic death-power to victory. Antichrist moves the earthly elements and even the forces of the heavens. However, death can strip nothing from the sovereignty of Christ's spirit, from his authority over all earth existence. It is in accord with his own will that the cosmic powers rise up in the hour of Golgotha. He has said to the officers in Gethsemane, 'But this is your hour: Darkness rules' (Luke 22:53).

In the midst of the darkness a mystery was manifested on Golgotha which may be mentioned only with great reserve. The body which hung on the cross began to radiate light. In many country districts of Europe, in a field or at the roadside, one can find crucifixes with a gilded figure on a black wood cross. A momentous secret of Good Friday is living here in the naive wisdom of folklore. A mysterious brilliance broke through the dreadful noonday night. The sun of Christ revealed itself as the physical sun suffered eclipse. A ray of Easter already wove itself into the darkness of Good Friday.

The last of the Seven Words from the Cross, 'It is finished,' does not refer to the sufferings which have been surmounted, but to the complete conquest over the power of death which has been achieved. Whereas death casts into the banishment of 'the other side' the soul of a man whom it has mocked during his lifetime with the power of earthly matter, the Christ, in dying, goes directly to the earth. The blood streams from his wounds; his soul goes with it into the body of the earth. When blood streams out from a dying man, the blood and the soul go different ways; here the soul goes with the blood. Later, the body is lowered into the grave; the earth opens in an earthquake and takes into itself the body of Christ. When a human body given up by the soul is lowered into the grave, body and soul go different ways. Christ's soul goes the same way, to the earth. That is the great cosmic sacrifice of love which the Christ is able to accomplish for the whole of earth-existence, because death can no longer hinder him. The earth receives the body and blood of Christ, the great communion, and therewith the medicine for the spiritualizing of all material existence is incorporated into earth existence — 'the medicine that makes whole.'

John 19:28–42

The death

²⁸After this Jesus perceived in spirit: Everything is now nearing its goal and fulfilment, and, so that the word of scripture should be accomplished, he said, 'I thirst.' ²⁹There was a jar of vinegar standing there. And they soaked a sponge in vinegar, fixed it around a hyssop branch and held it to his mouth. ³⁰And when Jesus had taken the vinegar, he said, 'It has been fulfilled.' Then he bowed his head and breathed out his spirit.

³¹Since it was the Day of Preparation, the Jews did not want the bodies to remain on the cross, for that Sabbath was a great festival day. So they asked Pilate that their legs might be broken and that they should be taken down from the cross. ³²And so the soldiers came and broke the legs of first the one, and then the other, who had been crucified with him. ³³When they came to Jesus and saw that he had already died, they did not break his legs. ³⁴But one of the soldiers thrust a lance in his side, and at once blood and water flowed out. ³⁵He who saw it has testified to it, and his testimony is true. And he knows that he is speaking the truth, so that you also may find the way of faith. ³⁶All this happened so that the scripture should be fulfilled:

His bones shall not be broken

³⁷and also the other place in the scriptures:

They shall look on him whom they have pierced.

The burial

³⁸Then Joseph of Arimathea went to Pilate and asked him for permission to take down the body of Jesus from the cross. He was a disciple of Jesus, but kept it secret for fear of the Jews. Pilate gave him permission. And so he came and took down the body. ³⁹Nicodemus came also, who had first come to Jesus in the realm of night, and he brought about a hundred pounds of a mixture of myrrh and aloes. ⁴⁰And

Saturday in Holy Week

The body of the Christ has been laid in the tomb belonging to Joseph of Arimathea. Saturnine heaviness hangs in the air and the meaning of Saturn's day is fulfilled. It has always been the custom of the Sabbath, as Saturn's day, for the adherents of the Old Covenant to observe it as a strictly ordained day of death-like rest. Today is the Sabbath of all Sabbaths. It is as though a fighter had gone into a dark cavern to overcome a dragon. Will he return victoriously to the light of day?

In the dark midday hour of the previous day, when Christ on the cross bowed his head and expired, the veil of the Temple 'was torn in two.' Vistas were opened into the interior of the world. Archetypal pictures formed themselves in the saturnine twilight. Table and Cross summarize the events of the last two days. Now the Tomb is added as a third archetypal symbol.

From times immemorial tombs also served as altars; all divine worship proceeded originally from the worship of the dead. People went to the tombs when they wished to commune with the gods. The souls of the departed were intermediaries between men and the gods, for since the souls of the dead could appear at the tombs, other dwellers in the spiritual world could also be met there. This was so in far-distant ages, when death was still the brother of sleep and as yet had no terrifying power over humanity. Men were not so hopelessly bound to the substance of the earthly body during physical life. So after death they were not so separated from the plane of earth. The communion of

they took the body of Jesus and wrapped it in strips of linen
soaked with the balsam spices, according to the burial custom of the Jews. [41]At the place of the crucifixion there was
a garden, and in the garden there was a new tomb where no
one had ever been buried.

the earthly world with the spiritual world still happened like breathing in and breathing out.

In the course of millennia man entered deeper and deeper into embodiment. The more he united with earthly substance, the less was it possible for him to remain in connection with the earth after death. The gap between 'here' and 'there' became increasingly difficult to bridge. Existence after death became, as is said in the First Epistle of Peter, a prison. Humanity was in danger of being deprived of immortality, of consciousness enduring beyond death. In the realm of the dead the souls were spellbound in a state of numbness. When the Egyptians mummified their dead and prayed before the embalmed bodies, they expressed their urgent desire to hold fast to the ancient conditions. It was an attempt, despite the ever-widening gulf, to unite the souls of men with the bodily remains of earthly life. But the downward trend of destiny could not be checked and, as the pre-Christian centuries advanced, dread of death took hold of humanity. The Greek world is filled with horror of the realm of the dead; in the Old Testament the idea of immortality fades away altogether. A great religious current arose without a certainty of immortal life, and the belief of living on in one's descendants took its place.

Yet in the pre-Christian centuries souls did not live nearly so heavily in the body as they do today. Hence those who were living on earth felt the tragic fate brought on by death as an oppressive burden. Though people still went to the tombs, the souls no longer came, and the gods were absent from the altars.

The feeling of anxiety in pre-Christian times derived far less from external conditions than from distress of soul. The earth seemed a parched land that had had no rain for a long time. Death became a terrifying spectre. This feeling lay at the root of the expectation of the Messiah which inspired all the peoples of pre-Christian times.

It was now between Holy Saturday and Easter. The body had been taken from the cross and laid in the grave. Providence ordained that cross and grave should stand on a spot which thousands of years before had been experienced as the centre of the earth. Between the rocky hill of Golgotha, which is a continuation of the lunar Mount Moriah, and the grave with its surrounding garden on Mount Zion, there was formerly a primal fissure in the earth's surface.* Ancient humanity saw in this the grave of Adam: here for the first time humanity was overcome by death. And so from very ancient times this primeval gorge, which splits Jerusalem into two parts, was believed to

---

* From the first to the fourth gospel the text contains an ever clearer revelation of the secret of Gethsemane. The first two gospels say only 'Jesus came with the disciples to a place called Gethsemane.' We assume that it was merely some unfamiliar spot. In Luke the text takes a new turn: 'And he left the house and went to the Mount of Olives as was his custom. And the disciples followed him.' It is not just any road, but one which leads to a spot where Jesus had often stayed. John's Gospel brings the full revelation: 'After these words Jesus left the house with his disciples and crossed over the Kidron brook. On the other side there was a garden which he and his disciples entered. This place was also known to Judas who betrayed him; for Jesus had often gathered his disciples around him there.' (18:1–2). Gethsemane is thus a place where esoteric instruction had been given to the disciples. The olive grove reached to the summit of the Mount of Olives. It was also the scene of the Little Apocalypse on the Tuesday evening of Passion week.

be the gate of the underworld. In this place the cross was erected and there today the Church of the Holy Sepulchre stands.

When now we try once more to find the inner aspect of events, it is as though the veil was rent before another sphere. The realm of the shades opens. In the saturnine darkness of this sphere an unexpected light is kindled. He who died upon the cross has entered the kingdom of the dead. One has come who is not subject to the magic compulsion of death, One who is free of all that dulls and deadens. He carries through death the full glory of his genius; and while on earth the dark Sabbath of the grave prevails, in the realm of the dead the sun rises. This is the meaning of Christ's descent into hell. In the kingdom of the departed a glimmer of hope lit up. The spell of death was loosened, and the prospect opened towards a future victory of the human soul over the spell of the underworld. While it was still Holy Saturday on earth, it was already Easter in the kingdom of the dead.

At the moment of Christ's death on Good Friday the earthquake began and it was still rumbling in the early hours of Easter morning. It did not cease fully all through Holy Saturday, though the powers of nature may have adapted themselves to the spell of the silence of the grave which belongs to this day. Rudolf Steiner has imparted from his spiritual investigations a certain fact which may be hard to accept, but which could be verified from a knowledge of the geological secrets which lie in the soil of Jerusalem. As a cosmic climax to the Mystery of Golgotha, the earthquake

tore open again the original fissure which had been
filled in the time of Solomon. And thus the whole
earth became the grave of the Christ. The earth took
deep into herself the Host that was administered to
her. When with the words of the creed as it is used
in the Christian Community, we express the event
of Holy Saturday, 'He was lowered into the grave
of the earth,' we touch upon the cosmic aspect of
the Mystery of Golgotha. It was the physical body
and the physical blood of the human being, Jesus
of Nazareth, which was the medicine received by
the earth. The sacramental stream which has gone
through humanity henceforward is linked to Easter.

It has been a right and valid principle that in all parts
of the Christian Church altars have always been formed
in the likeness of a tomb. Also the altars of the renewed
sacrament in the Christian Community have the form of
a tomb. And when the members of the congregation are
assembled round them, the principle of Holy Saturday
is always present. We are the ones waiting round the
sacred sepulchre, and at the table and tomb of the Lord
our dead can also draw near again. Those who have
inwardly united themselves in life with the renewed
sacrament can assuredly after death find their way to
this tomb more easily than to their own graves. Souls no
longer have any intensive relation to the cast-off body.
But when we are assembled round the altar, they can be
in our midst, and thereby strengthen our relationship
to the spiritual world. The new altars are surrounded
with the same play of archetypal pictures as was once
the grave in the precincts of the garden on Mount Zion.

The gulf is closed between this world and the other. The Easter garden begins to bloom in which our soul, like Mary Magdalene, can behold the Risen One as the gardener of a new world. The darkness of Saturn is lit up from within by the sun of Easter.

Easter joy

The Easter message is the heart and fountainhead of the Christian faith. The saying of Paul: 'If Christ did not rise again, then ... the power of our faith in your hearts is an illusion' (1Cor.15:14) justifies a description of Christianity simply as the religion of the Risen Christ. Christian devotion has ultimately no other purpose than this: to cherish community with the Risen Christ. Christ is not to be sought either in the past or in the future, but in the immediate present. His sphere is not a 'beyond;' he is near to us in this world in which we live.

Where is the sphere into which we must enter in order to feel and experience the nearness of the Risen Christ? Every year, during the Easter season, the hymnlike texts spoken at the altars of the Christian Community point to this sphere, and suggest at once its tremendous magnitude. A jubilant breath pervades the prayers of Easter, expressing itself twice, as with inward necessity, in the word 'rejoice.' Who rejoices? Who is made to rejoice by the Easter mysteries? In the first place the text says, 'the airy regions of the earth rejoice exceedingly,' and soon after, 'Christ has invaded man's rejoicing pulse of life.' First, the breathing soul-sphere of the whole planet rejoices, that renewed cosmic sphere of sunlit clouds, air and wind into which the earth grows in spring; then, the inward life of man, touched by the Risen Christ, rejoices too. We recognize the wide span of the soul at Easter; it comprises the outward and the inward world, macrocosm and microcosm.

Matthew 28:1–15

The Resurrection

When the Sabbath was over, in the early morning light of the first day of the week, Mary of Magdala and the other Mary came to see to the tomb. [2]And see, there was a great earthquake, the angel of the Lord descended from heaven, came and rolled the stone away and sat upon it. [3]His appearance was like lightning, and his garment was shining white like snow. [4]His presence terrified the guards; they trembled and fell down as if dead.

[5]And the angel said to the women, 'Have no fear. I know that you seek Jesus who was crucified. [6]He is not here. He has risen, as he himself said. Come and see the place where he lay. [7]Now go quickly to his disciples and say to them: He has risen from the dead and will lead you to Galilee where you will behold him. See, that is what I have to say to you.'

[8]Quickly they left the tomb, filled with both fear and joy, and they ran to take the message to the disciples. [9]And see, Jesus came to meet them and said: 'Greetings!' And they went up to him and took hold of his feet and fell down before him. [10]Then Jesus said to them, 'Have no fear! Go and give my brothers the message that they are to go to Galilee. There they will behold me.'

[11]While they were going, see, some of the guard went into the town and reported everything that had happened to the chief priests, [12]who then assembled together with the elders, and conferred. They gave the soldiers a substantial sum of money [13]and said, 'Tell people that his disciples came in the night and stole him away while you were asleep. [14]And if it comes to the governor's ears, we will talk with him and see to it that nothing happens to you.' [15]And they took the money and did as they were told, and this version has been handed down among the Jews to this day.

The fourfold Easter gospel

The artistic fourfoldness of the gospels meets us nowhere so vividly as in the Easter stories; here, the gospels are more differentiated in their special quality and colouring than anywhere else. They become four separate books, each with its individual character; and the synoptic harmony of the four, with all their differences and apparent contradictions, makes the universal totality of 'the gospel in the four gospels' appear with greatest clarity.

The composition of the Easter story in the Gospel of Matthew has a special grandeur. The first gospel completely surpasses the others in poetic design. A double drama, full of tension, frames the Easter scenes themselves. The cosmic drama of the earthquake prepares and attunes our soul from the beginning for the power and magnitude of the event. Only Matthew's Gospel mentions the shocks of the earthquake which, beginning with the afternoon of Good Friday, tore open the ground of the earth, and continued reverberating until the morning of Easter Sunday. The cosmic drama at the beginning is followed by a human drama at the end, the deception of the priests at the sepulchre of Joseph of Arimathea. The high priests have posted watchers because they are afraid of fraud; but now they themselves attempt a fraud, by inducing the watchers through bribes to make false statements. Then the story proceeds in terse and dramatic stages. The Easter scenes themselves begin at the tomb. This forms a prelude, which is also contained in the other

Mark 16:1–14

The Resurrection
And when the Sabbath was over, Mary Magdalene, Mary the mother of James, and Salome bought aromatic spices and took them to the tomb to anoint him.

²And at dawn on the first day of the week they came to the tomb, just as the sun was rising. ³And they said to one another, 'Who will roll away the stone for us from the entrance to the tomb?' ⁴And as they looked up, they saw that it had been rolled back; and the stone was very large.

⁵And they went into the tomb. There they saw a young man sitting on the right side, clad in a shining white garment. And they were beside themselves with amazement. ⁶Then he said to them, 'Do not be startled! You seek Jesus of Nazareth, the crucified one. He is risen and is not here. See, there is the place where they laid his body. ⁷Now go and say to his disciples and to Peter: "He will lead you to Galilee." There you will see him as he promised you.'

⁸And they fled from the tomb in great haste, for they were trembling with agitation, and their souls were as if transported, and, being awestruck, they were unable to say anything to anyone about what they had experienced.

The appearance of the Risen One
⁹When he had risen, early on the first day of the week, he appeared first to Mary of Magdala, from whom he had driven out seven demons. ¹⁰And she went and proclaimed it to those who had walked with him and who were now sunk in tears and lamenting. ¹¹When they heard: He lives and she has seen him, their hearts could not grasp it. ¹²After this he revealed himself, transformed in appearance, to two of them on the way as they were walking over the fields. ¹³And they came and proclaimed it to the others; but they could not open their hearts to their words either.

¹⁴Finally he appeared to the eleven themselves as they

three gospels. Afterwards, we are taken at once to the
summit of a high mountain. The angel at the tomb has
asked the women to tell the disciples that the Risen
Christ will go before them into Galilee; and now we
also are immediately in Galilee. Together with the disciples we are transported to a height from which the
world can be surveyed as if we were on the summit of
that marvellous mountain where once the three most
intimate disciples saw the Christ in his transfigured
glory: on the summit of Tabor, the mountain of mountains, which rises in the sunny landscape of Galilee.
Here, the Risen One speaks to his disciples: 'Now all
creative power in heaven and on the earth has been
given me;' and he sends his disciples as apostles into
all the kingdoms of the world.

In Mark, the framework of the external dramatic
events is missing; an inward dramatic quality takes its
place. After the meeting with the angel at the tomb, we
see the women return to the room where the disciples
are united. It is the Cenacle, the room of the washing
of the feet and the Last Supper; the sacred, time-hon-
oured place on Mount Zion; the centre of the spiritual
history of humanity from times immemorial. In this
room the events of Easter continue. Here the Risen
One enters the circle of the disciples and, speaking to
them, conquers their hardened hearts. Having been at
first without understanding for the Easter message,
and even for the words of the Risen Christ, they can
now become bearers of the cosmic impulse which has
come into the world through the Resurrection. And
now they experience how the Christ is raised before

were celebrating the meal. And he reprimanded them for their lack of openness and for their hardness of heart, because they had not wanted to believe those who had seen him, the Risen One.

Luke 24:1–12

The Resurrection

But on the first day of the week, at the very first glimmering of dawn, they came to the tomb with the aromatic extracts that they had prepared. ²And they found the stone rolled away from the tomb, ³but when they went into the tomb they did not find the body of Jesus, the Lord. ⁴And while they stood there, completely at a loss, suddenly two men were standing before them in raiment which shone like continuous lightning. ⁵They were overcome by terror and they bowed their faces to the ground. Then those beings said to them, 'Why do you seek the Living One among the dead? He is not here, he has risen. ⁶Remember the words that he spoke while he was still in Galilee: ⁷The Son of Man must be betrayed and delivered into the hands of sinful men and be crucified; but on the third day he will rise.' ⁸And they remembered his words ⁹and returned home from the tomb and proclaimed all this to the eleven and the others who belonged to his circle. ¹⁰It was Mary of Magdala and Joanna and Mary the mother of James; they and the other women who were with them told this to the apostles. ¹¹But it seemed to them like empty talk; they did not believe them.

John 20:1–10

The Resurrection

On the first day after the Sabbath at the first breaking of the day, Mary of Magdala comes to the tomb and sees that the stone has been taken away. ²And she runs and comes to Simon

their eyes into heavenly heights, although they remain in the house; a first glimpse of the Ascension moves them within the four walls of the room.

Now we begin to see the deeper symbolism in the Easter stories, which belong together: Matthew leads to the top of the mountain, Mark leads into the house. In contrast to the dramatic study of Matthew, a great and wonderful inwardness lives in the Gospel of Luke. The transition from outside to inside which takes place in passing from the first to the second gospel is further deepened. This transition dominates the story of the two disciples who walk to Emmaus, which follows the scene at the tomb. For these disciples, too, the real meeting with the Risen One, by which they recognize him, occurs only at the moment when they have entered the house at the end of the way and have sat down at the table at twilight, in the stillness of the house. The theme of the transition from outside to inside is continued here; at a quick pace we return with the two disciples on the same evening to Jerusalem, and enter with them into the Cenacle, where the other disciples are assembled; and we are made witnesses of the Risen One appearing suddenly in the midst of the disciples and taking food and drink before their eyes, in order to unite himself with them in the sacred meal. In Luke, as in Mark, the interior of the house is the scene of the real Easter meeting, following the prelude at the tomb; but the scenes of the inward drama in Luke have more soul and are more richly differentiated.

John presents us with a very great wealth of Easter scenes. Even the prelude at the tomb develops into a

Peter and to the other disciple whom Jesus loved, and says to them, 'They have taken the Lord out of the tomb, and we do not know where they have laid him.' ³And so Peter and the other disciple set off towards the tomb. ⁴They both ran, and the other disciple ran faster and overtook Peter and came to the tomb first. ⁵He bent forward and saw the linen cloths lying there, but he did not go in. ⁶Then Simon Peter, who was following him, also came, and he went straight into the tomb. And he beheld the linen cloths lying there ⁷and the veil which had been over his head; it was, however, not lying with the cloths but bundled up in one particular place. ⁸Then the other disciple also went in, he who had come first to the tomb; and he understood, and faith entered his heart, giving certainty to his soul. ⁹For as yet they had not grasped the meaning of the word of scripture, that he would rise from the dead. ¹⁰And the disciples went again to their house.

whole drama. Mary Magdalene comes to the tomb; no angel is there to mitigate the shock which she feels at the sight of the empty tomb. She walks back all the way to find the disciples. Two of the disciples, seized with great anxiety, run through the whole city until they come to the tomb, but they also find it empty; no spiritual figure appears to them; they have to leave, taking with them an apparently insoluble riddle; in silence they return to the Cenacle. Mary Magdalene is left alone at the tomb. Only now, when she stands at the tomb for the second time, her soul is opened up for the presence of spiritual beings who are there; and the first meeting with the angels grows into the first meeting with the Risen One himself who appears to her as the gardener. And once more, but now charged with increasing content, the transition from outside to inside takes place. We find ourselves again within the room of the Last Supper, and share in the experience of how the Risen One manifests himself to the disciples. The following scenes develop with such rich detail that we begin to recognize how the Easter fellowship of the disciples with the Risen One extends beyond Easter Sunday, and fills the whole season. One week after, Thomas, the doubter, is permitted to convince himself through physical touch of the fact of the bodily resurrection. But the sequence in John is not yet at an end; the steps which have led us from outside to inside are reversed. The gospel leads us again outward. The interior scenes are followed by a series of scenes which take place under the open sky of Galilee. All of a sudden, the disciples are transported to the Sea of Galilee.

During the night, they draw in the miraculous draught
of fishes; and in the cool of the morning, on the shores
of the blue lake, the radiant figure of the Risen One
appears to them. A holy meal unites them with him.
Then he addresses three times his earnest quesion to
Peter; eventually he gives to the disciples their apos-
tolic charge, pointing into the far distant future with
mysterious words.

We can now discern an important aspect in the
wonderful composition of the gospels as a whole. In
the scenes which follow the prelude at the tomb, we
are led, in the sequence of Matthew to John, through
three archetypal settings: on the mountain, in the
house and on the sea. Apparently physical landscape
is described, but in fact we are shown regions of the
soul which we have to traverse in order to meet the
Risen One. The Gospel, taken in its entirety in the four
gospels, has given the first pictorial hint of his sphere.

The angels at the tomb

Most Bible readers take it that the Easter stories in all four gospels agree in describing first the meeting with the angels at the tomb. But this is not so.

The Gospel of Matthew says that the women come to the grave and in the early light of dawn receive a severe shock, for the earthquake, which seemed to have subsided for a whole day, breaks out afresh. They have to make their way among trembling rocks. Then a flash of lightning tears away the curtain, as it were, from the world of the senses. When they reach the grave, a spirit-form shines before them in over-whelming brilliance. 'When the Sabbath was over, in the early morning light of the first day of the week, Mary of Magdala and the other Mary came to see to the tomb. And see, there was a great earthquake, the angel of the Lord descended from heaven, came and rolled the stone away and sat upon it. His appearance was like lightning, and his garment was shining white like snow.' (Matt.28:1). When the lightning has struck the watchers to the ground, the angel speaks to the women. The first premonition of Easter is given them, and they receive a message enjoining the disciples to go to Galilee.

In the light of the supersensory conception of the world which is the basis of the gospels, the earthquake is described, not as a natural process, but as the activity of supersensory powers and beings. Through the souls of the women we, too, see a powerful being from the angelic hierarchies taking part. An angel who resembles the powers of lightning and of snow descends from heaven to roll away the stone. It is important to note that the women perceive the angel while they are still outside the tomb. The vision that overtakes them is mingled with the physical perception that the entry to the tomb is exposed by the rolling away of the stone which has covered it. The supersensory experiences which the gospels recount are never arbitrary, but have a firm psychological basis. Even in the gospels people do not have supersensory experiences without some cause. In every case a specific emotion is active in the soul which releases the vision. According to the description in the Gospel of Matthew an overwhelming shock brought it about that suddenly, as the rock split, not only the outer event but also the supersensory being, the angel of the earthquake, was perceived.

In the Gospel of Mark the account of the meeting of the women with the angel is different, both in its inner aspect, and in the circumstances of its place and time. On their way to the tomb the women are full of anxiety as to how they will be able to get into the closed sepulchre. But as they reach the end of their journey they are greatly surprised to find that the stone has been rolled away, and that the entrance to the tomb is open. The problem that has worried them has been solved, but such a solution must prepare them for still further and perhaps greater surprises. Mark's comment, 'for the stone was very large,' makes us share in the women's breathless astonishment. They go inside the tomb, and there a bright light streams towards them out of the darkness. On their right they see an angelic form in a long white garment. The angel, who is described as a young man, speaks to them of the Resurrection, and gives them the message for the disciples about Galilee.

This experience of the angel does not occur as in the Gospel of Matthew, before they enter the tomb, but inside it, and it happens also at a somewhat later point of time. While Matthew describes the angelic being as 'the angel of the Lord,' which in Hebrew would read 'the angel of Yahweh,' Mark speaks of the 'young man' who sits to the right of the tomb. This is an entirely different situation and it is also a different condition which releases the vision. This time it is not fear but astonishment. Here is a first apparent contradiction between the two gospels.

In the Gospel of Luke things progress still further before the experience occurs that leads out of the sphere of sense-perception into the supersensory. The description of the external situation is carried to the point to which it had been taken by St Mark. The women come to the grave; they find the stone rolled away from the entrance and go inside. They search for the dead body of Jesus. And the longer they search, the more anxious and disturbed they become because they cannot find him. Only when their anxiety has reached its climax are their eyes opened to the spiritual beings who are there. 'And while they stood there, completely at a loss, suddenly two men were standing before them in raiment which shone like continuous lightning. They were overcome by terror and they bowed their faces to the ground.' (Luke 24:4f).

In this case the women have penetrated many

paces deeper into the tomb than in the account given
by Mark, and have already been there for some time.
Now it is not fear of the earthquake, nor astonishment
over the open tomb, but their anxiety over the empty
grave which releases the vision. The feeling which
goes beyond sense-perception is quite different and
belongs to a more advanced consciousness. This time,
surprisingly, it is two angel beings who reveal themselves to the women, and instead of being called 'angel
of the Lord' or 'young man,' they are now called 'two
men in white raiment.'

By this time it is obvious that there is nothing
haphazard in these discrepancies between the sev-
eral gospels, but that the advance from one gospel
to the next follows a specific law. The meetings with
the angels undergo such an orderly transformation,
a metamorphosis so significant, that the differences
in the gospels, taken as a whole, draw attention to a
special secret.

This becomes specially clear when we come to the
Gospel of John. Here, Mary Magdalene comes alone
to the tomb. She enters and finds it empty. Thus the
external course of events is once more taken up at the
point reached in the preceding gospel. The feelings
that had been stirred in the soul of Mary Magdalene
by the earthquake, the open tomb and the empty
grave are not described. The Fourth Gospel is concerned with experiences which take place later. Mary
Magdalene leaves the tomb without having met with
an angel. She goes all the way back through the city
to the disciples. Now Peter and John run to the tomb,

and with her they peer into the empty grave. Although there is no direct mention of this in the gospel, it is in accordance with the spirit of the Gospel of John to suppose that the disciples saw something of the cosmic aspect of the empty grave. On the site of the tomb the earthquake had reopened a deep cleft which formed part of the ancient chasm in the ground of Jerusalem which had been levelled by Solomon.* Thus the disciples not only look into the empty grave, they look into a gloomy chasm. They have a unique experience of the mystical stage called 'standing before the abyss.' Bewildered, they go away again, and Mary Magdalene remains there alone. Some time elapses. Then Mary Magdalene weeps. The tears that she now sheds are due neither to fright, nor to astonishment or anxiety. She weeps because she is wholly absorbed in love for him who has been torn away from her. Much more has happened than that Jesus has died. All the miraculous and inexplicable events since midday on Good Friday awaken dreamlike perceptions, whereby the greatness of him who has passed through death stands before the soul of Mary Magdalene as never before. The more she feels his greatness, the greater is her love. This love opens the eyes of her soul. While her physical sight is blinded with tears, her weeping awakens spiritual sight, and she perceives two figures. But these are not the same as those described by Luke. She sees two angels in white garments, one at the head and one at the foot of the place where the body of Jesus had been laid. Although there is still no trace of the beloved body, yet now, through her spiritual experience, she is conscious of the exact spot where he had lain. The two angels say to her, 'Woman, why are you weeping?' In that moment, as she collects herself to answer them, the experience moves forward to a new stage. She turns round, and there, in Joseph of Arimathea's garden, she sees a figure facing the tomb. She does not recognize him as Jesus. He who stands outside appears to her in the form of a gardener. And her first impulse is to ask him if he can tell her whither the body of Jesus has vanished. Then Jesus speaks to her in the very same words which earlier the angels had used, 'Woman, why are you weeping?'

We should not think that either the angel or the Risen One speaks in human language. What is heard inwardly by the soul is reproduced by the gospel in human words. It is only by silencing the human words that we can hope to enter into the inner hearing from which they come. In the Gospel of John it is out of the inner hearing of the question put by the angels that the new spiritual meeting arises whereby Mary Magdalene becomes the first bearer of the real Easter perception. The figure out there facing the tomb takes, as it were, the words from the angels' mouths.

Again, the figure that Mary Magdalene sees as a continuation of her perception of the angels is clearly that of a man. When the gospel says that she thought it was the gardener, this does not mean that she was deceived. Jesus does appear to her as a gardener. The medieval painters, by representing the Risen Christ as a gardener, have adequately reproduced the imagination which passed before Mary Magdalene's soul. The

Risen One is really the gardener of a new garden, the planter and cultivator of a new life on earth.

The sight of the gardener brings new hope to her loving soul. Perhaps he who appears before her can restore to her the lost one. Only a few moments ago, love of Christ had caused her tears to flow. Now that same love lights up her soul. At that moment she feels herself called by name, and at last understands that it is Christ who stands before her in the Easter garden. She has really found again him who had been wrested from her. She puts out her hands to embrace him. But the stern warning meets her 'Do not touch me!' The Easter mystery is not yet consummated. What happens at the tomb takes place only in the forecourt. The complete manifestation of the Risen One in his spirit-body is first experienced only when the outdoor scenes have come to an end, and the indoor scenes within the circle of the disciples have begun.

The Gospel of John carries further the metamorphosis of the Easter prelude at the tomb. The significant transformations and amplifications in the meetings with the angels of the first three gospels here reach their climax. After the terror of the earthquake, the amazement at the open tomb, the anxiety over the empty grave, it is now tears of love which open the eye of Mary Magdalene's soul for the angels. Then the meeting with the gardener forms the transition from the angelic forecourt to the actual temple of Easter.

The Three Years

The Life of Christ between Baptism and Ascension

Emil Bock

How can a scientifically-minded person approach the healings and miracles of the Gospels, including such events as the raising of Lazarus and the Resurrection itself?

Emil Bock rediscovers the works of Christ without minimizing the difficulties. He brings together historical records and the geographical background of the Gospels, all the while keeping sight of their spiritual wisdom.

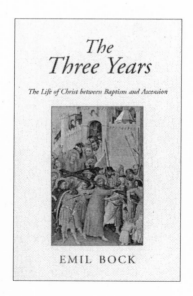

florisbooks.co.uk

Studies in the Gospels

Volumes 1 & 2

Emil Bock

In the course of his pioneering work in The Christian Community, Emil Bock made many studies of different aspects of the Gospels. Bringing his wide knowledge of the history of that time together with his deep insights in anthroposophy, he brings a fresh view of the familiar stories of the New Testament.

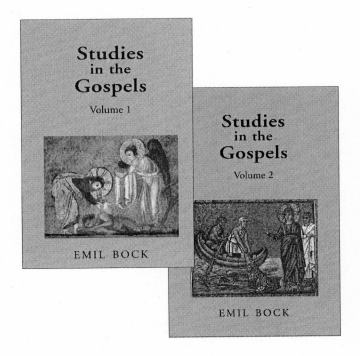

florisbooks.co.uk

The Childhood of Jesus

The Unknown Years

Emil Bock

The Gospels of Matthew and Luke have many discrepancies in their account of the genealogy and nativity of Jesus. Bock reveals that there were two families and two 'Jesus boys' whose destinies were to combine and be fulfilled through the divine plan.

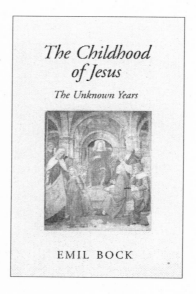

florisbooks.co.uk